MAD LIBS®

FOR PRESIDENT

By Roger Price and Leonard Stern

SCHOLASTIC INC.

New York Toronto London Auckland Sydney
Mexico City New Delhi Hong Kong Buenos Aires

ISBN 0-439-69679-8

22 21 20 19 18 17 16   10 11 12 13 14 15 16/0

Printed in the U.S.A.   40

First Scholastic printing, September 2004

MAD LIBS
INSTRUCTIONS

MAD LIBS® is a game for people who don't like games! It can be played by one, two, three, four, or forty.

• RIDICULOUSLY SIMPLE DIRECTIONS

In this tablet you will find stories containing blank spaces where words are left out. One player, the READER, selects one of these stories. The READER does not tell anyone what the story is about. Instead, he/she asks the other players, the WRITERS, to give him/her words. These words are used to fill in the blank spaces in the story.

• TO PLAY

The READER asks each WRITER in turn to call out a word—an adjective or a noun or whatever the space calls for—and uses them to fill in the blank spaces in the story. The result is a MAD LIBS® game.

When the READER then reads the completed MAD LIBS® game to the other players, they will discover that they have written a story that is fantastic, screamingly funny, shocking, silly, crazy, or just plain dumb—depending upon which words each WRITER called out.

• EXAMPLE (*Before* and *After*)

"_____!" he said _____
    EXCLAMATION   ADVERB

as he jumped into his convertible _____ and
                                      NOUN

drove off with his _____ wife.
                   ADJECTIVE

"*Ouch!*_____!" he said *Stupidly*_____
    EXCLAMATION   ADVERB

as he jumped into his convertible *cat* and
                                        NOUN

drove off with his *brave* wife.
                   ADJECTIVE

In case you have forgotten what adjectives, adverbs, nouns, and verbs are, here is a quick review:

An ADJECTIVE describes something or somebody. *Lumpy, soft, ugly, messy,* and *short* are adjectives.

An ADVERB tells how something is done. It modifies a verb and usually ends in "ly." *Modestly, stupidly, greedily,* and *carefully* are adverbs.

A NOUN is the name of a person, place or thing. *Sidewalk, umbrella, bridle, bathtub,* and *nose* are nouns.

A VERB is an action word. *Run, pitch, jump,* and *swim* are verbs. Put the verbs in past tense if the directions say PAST TENSE. *Ran, pitched, jumped,* and *swam* are verbs in the past tense.

When we ask for A PLACE, we mean any sort of place: a country or city *(Spain, Cleveland)* or a room *(bathroom, kitchen).*

An EXCLAMATION or SILLY WORD is any sort of funny sound, gasp, grunt, or outcry, like *Wow!, Ouch!, Whomp!, Ick!,* and *Gadzooks!*

When we ask for specific words, like a NUMBER, a COLOR, an ANIMAL, or a PART OF THE BODY, we mean a word that is one of those things, like *seven, blue, horse,* or *head.*

When we ask for a PLURAL, it means more than one. For example, *cat* pluralized is *cats.*

MAD LIBS® is fun to play with friends, but you can also play it by yourself! To begin with, DO NOT look at the story on the page below. Fill in the blanks on this page with the words called for. Then, using the words you have selected, fill in the blank spaces in the story.

Now you've created your own hilarious MAD LIBS® game!

GEORGE WASHINGTON

NOUN _____

ADJECTIVE _____

ADJECTIVE _____

NOUN _____

NOUN _____

EXCLAMATION _____

VERB (PAST TENSE) _____

NOUN _____

NOUN _____

NOUN _____

NOUN _____

NOUN _____

OCCUPATION _____

MAD LIBS
GEORGE WASHINGTON

George Washington, the Father of our _____, was a very
                                        NOUN

_____ man. When George was a/an _____ boy,
   ADJECTIVE   ADJECTIVE

he took his _____ and chopped down his father's favorite
                 NOUN

cherry _____. "_____!" said his father. "Who
          NOUN   EXCLAMATION

has _____ my _____?" Then he saw George
   VERB (PAST TENSE)   NOUN

holding a sharp _____ in his hand. "Father," said George,
                      NOUN

"I cannot tell a lie. I did it with my little _____." His father
                                                    NOUN

smiled and patted little George on the _____. "You are a very
                                              NOUN

honest _____," he said, "and some day you may become the
            NOUN

first _____ of the United States."
        OCCUPATION

MAD LIBS® is fun to play with friends, but you can also play it by yourself! To begin with, DO NOT look at the story on the page below. Fill in the blanks on this page with the words called for. Then, using the words you have selected, fill in the blank spaces in the story.

Now you've created your own hilarious MAD LIBS® game!

MAD LIBS ON DIPLOMACY

ARTICLE OF CLOTHING (PLURAL) _____

ADJECTIVE _____

ADJECTIVE _____

PLURAL NOUN _____

ADJECTIVE _____

PLURAL NOUN _____

ADJECTIVE _____

VERB ENDING IN "ING" _____

VERB _____

PLURAL NOUN _____

ADJECTIVE _____

PLURAL NOUN _____

PART OF THE BODY (PLURAL) _____

NOUN _____

PLURAL NOUN _____

ADJECTIVE _____

PLURAL NOUN _____

NOUN _____

MAD LIBS

MAD LIBS ON DIPLOMACY

One of the many _____ that the president wears
_{ARTICLE OF CLOTHING (PLURAL)}

is that of the diplomat. Diplomacy requires _____ character
_{ADJECTIVE}

and a/an _____ demeanor. Because the president will be
_{ADJECTIVE}

meeting _____-of-state from many countries, it is important
_{PLURAL NOUN}

that he/she learns all there is to know about the _____ cultural
_{ADJECTIVE}

differences between _____. The president must observe
_{PLURAL NOUN}

the _____ customs when _____ abroad.
_{ADJECTIVE}   _{VERB ENDING IN "ING"}

He may have to _____ before kings and _____; he
_{VERB}   _{PLURAL NOUN}

may have to sit on the _____ ground with his _____
_{ADJECTIVE}   _{PLURAL NOUN}

folded under him and eat with his _____; he may
_{PART OF THE BODY (PLURAL)}

even have to speak in a foreign _____. By observing the
_{NOUN}

_____ of other countries, the president sets a/an _____
_{PLURAL NOUN}   _{ADJECTIVE}

example for American _____ who visit another _____.
_{PLURAL NOUN}   _{NOUN}

MAD LIBS® is fun to play with friends, but you can also play it by yourself! To begin with, DO NOT look at the story on the page below. Fill in the blanks on this page with the words called for. Then, using the words you have selected, fill in the blank spaces in the story.

Now you've created your own hilarious MAD LIBS® game!

THE CONSTITUTION

ADJECTIVE_____

PLURAL NOUN _____

ADJECTIVE_____

PLURAL NOUN _____

ADJECTIVE_____

PLURAL NOUN _____

PLURAL NOUN _____

PLURAL NOUN _____

PLURAL NOUN _____

ADJECTIVE_____

PLURAL NOUN _____

ADJECTIVE_____

PLURAL NOUN _____

MAD LIBS
THE CONSTITUTION

Studying the Constitution is a/an _____ rainy day camp
ADJECTIVE

activity. In 1787, a convention of important American _____
PLURAL NOUN

ratified our Constitution. The Constitution was a/an _____
ADJECTIVE

document that guaranteed that the U.S. would not merely be a

league of independent _____, but a nation with a/an
PLURAL NOUN

_____ government that would deal with _____
ADJECTIVE   PLURAL NOUN

as well as _____. The Constitution provided for a
PLURAL NOUN

senate, to which every state would send two _____, and
PLURAL NOUN

a larger body called the House of _____, which was based
PLURAL NOUN

on population. The government was divided into three branches:

the judicial, the legislative, and the _____. This created
ADJECTIVE

a system of checks and _____ that works to protect us to
PLURAL NOUN

this day and gives us our _____ government of the
ADJECTIVE

people, for the people, and by the _____.
PLURAL NOUN

From MAD LIBS® FOR PRESIDENT • Copyright © 2004, 2000 by Price Stern Sloan,
a division of Penguin Young Readers Group, 345 Hudson Street, New York, New York 10014.

MAD LIBS® is fun to play with friends, but you can also play it by yourself. To begin with, DO NOT look at the story on the page below. Fill in the blanks on this page with the words called for. Then, using the words you have selected, fill in the blank spaces in the story.

Now you've created your own hilarious MAD LIBS® game!

POLITICAL SPEECH

ADJECTIVE _____

ADJECTIVE _____

PLURAL NOUN _____

PLURAL NOUN _____

ADJECTIVE _____

NOUN _____

NOUN _____

PLURAL NOUN _____

ADJECTIVE _____

PERSON IN ROOM (MALE) _____

ADJECTIVE _____

NOUN _____

ADJECTIVE _____

NOUN _____

PLURAL NOUN _____

PLURAL NOUN _____

ADJECTIVE _____

ADJECTIVE _____

ADJECTIVE _____

MAD LIBS
POLITICAL SPEECH

Ladies and gentlemen, on this _____ occasion it is a privilege
ADJECTIVE

to address such a/an _____-looking group of _____.
ADJECTIVE   PLURAL NOUN

I can tell from your smiling _____ that you will support my
PLURAL NOUN

_____ program in the coming election. I promise that, if
ADJECTIVE

elected, there will be a/an _____ in every _____ and
NOUN   NOUN

two _____ in every garage. I want to warn you against my
PLURAL NOUN

_____ opponent, Mr. _____. The man is
ADJECTIVE   PERSON IN ROOM (MALE)

nothing but a/an _____ _____. He has a/an
ADJECTIVE   NOUN

_____ character and is working _____ in glove with the
ADJECTIVE   NOUN

criminal element. If elected, I promise to eliminate vice. I will keep

the _____ off the city's streets. I will keep crooks from
PLURAL NOUN

dipping their _____ in the public till. I promise you
PLURAL NOUN

_____ government, _____ taxes, and _____ schools.
ADJECTIVE   ADJECTIVE   ADJECTIVE

MAD LIBS® is fun to play with friends, but you can also play it by yourself! To begin with, DO NOT look at the story on the page below. Fill in the blanks on this page with the words called for. Then, using the words you have selected, fill in the blank spaces in the story.

Now you've created your own hilarious MAD LIBS® game!

SPEAKING OF SPEAKING

ADJECTIVE _____

VERB ENDING IN "ING" _____

PLURAL NOUN _____

NOUN _____

PLURAL NOUN _____

ADJECTIVE _____

PLURAL NOUN _____

PLURAL NOUN _____

NOUN _____

NOUN _____

PART OF THE BODY _____

ADJECTIVE _____

ADJECTIVE _____

PART OF THE BODY _____

TYPE OF LIQUID _____

PART OF THE BODY _____

MAD LIBS
SPEAKING OF SPEAKING

A recent _____ poll shows that the majority of people are
ADJECTIVE

terrified of public _____. They would rather walk
VERB ENDING IN "ING"

across burning _____ or swim in _____-infested
PLURAL NOUN NOUN

waters than give a speech in front of a group of _____. This
PLURAL NOUN

_____ fear can be overcome in five easy _____:
ADJECTIVE PLURAL NOUN

1. Organize all of your _____ on a piece of _____:
PLURAL NOUN NOUN

2. Remember to start your speech with a funny _____.
NOUN

3. When speaking, look your audience straight in the _____
PART OF THE BODY

and speak in a strong and _____ voice.
ADJECTIVE

4. Be simple. Never use _____ words that are over the
ADJECTIVE

audience's _____.
PART OF THE BODY

5. Always keep a pitcher of _____ next to you, in case your
TYPE OF LIQUID

_____ goes dry.
PART OF THE BODY

MAD LIBS® is fun to play with friends, but you can also play it by yourself! To begin with, DO NOT look at the story on the page below. Fill in the blanks on this page with the words called for. Then, using the words you have selected, fill in the blank spaces in the story.

Now you've created your own hilarious MAD LIBS® game!

MOUNT RUSHMORE

ADJECTIVE_____

NOUN _____

VERB (PAST TENSE)_____

NOUN _____

PART OF THE BODY (PLURAL) _____

PLURAL NOUN _____

PLURAL NOUN _____

PLURAL NOUN _____

PART OF THE BODY (PLURAL) _____

RELATIVE _____

NOUN _____

NOUN _____

VERB ENDING IN "ING" _____

NUMBER _____

NOUN _____

VERB _____

MAD LIBS

MOUNT RUSHMORE

In the _____ Hills of South Dakota, a/an _____
      ADJECTIVE   NOUN

named Gutzon Borglum _____ a/an _____ to
                           VERB (PAST TENSE)   NOUN

resemble the _____ of four U.S. presidents. Using
                   PART OF THE BODY (PLURAL)

_____ and _____, the sculptors would chip away
   PLURAL NOUN   PLURAL NOUN

tons of _____ until the _____ of
        PLURAL NOUN   PART OF THE BODY (PLURAL)

the presidents emerged. The presidents include George Washington,

the _____ of our country; Abraham Lincoln, who preserved
        RELATIVE

the _____; Thomas Jefferson, author of the Declaration
        NOUN

of _____; and Theodore Roosevelt, who was famous for
     NOUN

_____ up San Juan Hill in the Spanish-American War.
VERB ENDING IN "ING"

More than _____ tourists from all over the _____
          NUMBER   NOUN

_____ Mount Rushmore each year.
    VERB

From MAD LIBS® FOR PRESIDENT • Copyright © 2004, 2000 by Price Stern Sloan,
a division of Penguin Young Readers Group, 345 Hudson Street, New York, New York 10014.

MAD LIBS® is fun to play with friends, but you can also play it by yourself! To begin with, DO NOT look at the story on the page below. Fill in the blanks on this page with the words called for. Then, using the words you have selected, fill in the blank spaces in the story.

Now you've created your own hilarious MAD LIBS® game!

THE GETTYSBURG ADDRESS

PLURAL NOUN _____

NOUN _____

ADJECTIVE _____

PLURAL NOUN _____

ADJECTIVE _____

NOUN _____

SAME NOUN _____

ADJECTIVE _____

FAMOUS PERSON _____

PLURAL NOUN _____

SAME PLURAL NOUN _____

SAME PLURAL NOUN _____

NOUN _____

MAD LIBS®
THE GETTYSBURG ADDRESS

Four score and seven years ago, our _____ brought forth
                                     PLURAL NOUN

on this _____ a/an _____ nation, conceived in
            NOUN   ADJECTIVE

liberty and dedicated to the proposition that all _____
                                                   PLURAL NOUN

are created _____. Now we are engaged in a great civil
              ADJECTIVE

war, testing whether that _____ or any _____ so
                             NOUN   SAME NOUN

conceived and so dedicated to the _____ task remaining
                                    ADJECTIVE

before us . . . so that this nation, under _____ , shall
                                            FAMOUS PERSON

have a new birth of freedom, and that government of the

_____ , by the _____ , and for the
   PLURAL NOUN   SAME PLURAL NOUN

_____ shall not perish from the _____ .
   SAME PLURAL NOUN   NOUN

From MAD LIBS® FOR PRESIDENT • Copyright © 2004, 2000 by Price Stern Sloan,
a division of Penguin Young Readers Group, 345 Hudson Street, New York, New York 10014.

MAD LIBS® is fun to play with friends, but you can also play it by yourself! To begin with, DO NOT look at the story on the page below. Fill in the blanks on this page with the words called for. Then, using the words you have selected, fill in the blank spaces in the story.

Now you've created your own hilarious MAD LIBS® game!

A GREAT DEBATE

PLURAL NOUN _____

NUMBER _____

VERB _____

NUMBER _____

VERB _____

NOUN _____

PLURAL NOUN _____

PLURAL NOUN _____

VERB _____

VERB _____

ADJECTIVE_____

NUMBER _____

NOUN _____

VERB ENDING IN "ING" _____

NOUN _____

PLURAL NOUN _____

MAD LIBS
A GREAT DEBATE

MODERATOR: Good evening, ladies, _____, and candi-
                 _{PLURAL NOUN}

dates. Each candidate will have _____ minutes
                                _{NUMBER}

to _____ and _____ seconds for rebuttal.
   _{VERB}   _{NUMBER}

After that time, you will not be able to _____.
                                          _{VERB}

Our first question goes to Candidate #1: Describe

your views on _____ reform.
               _{NOUN}

CANDIDATE #1: I believe that the choice of _____ should be
                                               _{PLURAL NOUN}

given back to the American _____. I say,
                            _{PLURAL NOUN}

let the people _____!
                _{VERB}

MODERATOR: Candidate #2, would you like to _____?
                                                  _{VERB}

CANDIDATE #2: My opponent would like you to believe that he is

being _____, but in fact, we would need
       _{ADJECTIVE}

a/an _____-dollar increase in _____
      _{NUMBER}   _{NOUN}

taxes in order to fund his plan. Once again, he is

_____ the real _____.
_{VERB ENDING IN "ING"}   _{NOUN}

MODERATOR: Thank you, candidates. And now a few words from

our _____.
     _{PLURAL NOUN}

From MAD LIBS® FOR PRESIDENT • Copyright © 2004, 2000 by Price Stern Sloan,
a division of Penguin Young Readers Group, 345 Hudson Street, New York, New York 10014.

MAD LIBS® is fun to play with friends, but you can also play it by yourself! To begin with, DO NOT look at the story on the page below. Fill in the blanks on this page with the words called for. Then, using the words you have selected, fill in the blank spaces in the story.

Now you've created your own hilarious MAD LIBS® game!

FOURTH OF JULY

NUMBER _____

MONTH _____

ADJECTIVE _____

NOUN _____

ADJECTIVE _____

NOUN _____

NOUN _____

ADJECTIVE _____

PLURAL NOUN _____

PLURAL NOUN _____

PLURAL NOUN _____

ADJECTIVE _____

NOUN _____

NOUN _____

NOUN _____

PLURAL NOUN _____

PLURAL NOUN _____

PLURAL NOUN _____

ADJECTIVE _____

ADVERB _____

VERB _____

PLURAL NOUN _____

NOUN _____

MAD LIBS
FOURTH OF JULY

Every year on the _____ th of _____ , we celebrate the Fourth
                   NUMBER   MONTH

of July. This holiday commemorates the birth of our _____
                                                          ADJECTIVE

_____ . Many _____ citizens observe
     NOUN   ADJECTIVE

Independence _____ by hanging their _____
                  NOUN   NOUN

from a window or by running it up a/an _____ pole.
                                            ADJECTIVE

Most _____ spend this holiday at home with family and
       PLURAL NOUN

_____ or visit national _____ or _____
  PLURAL NOUN   PLURAL NOUN   ADJECTIVE

beaches. Food as American as apple _____ , hamburgers,
                                         NOUN

and corn on the _____ are traditional holiday _____ .
                     NOUN   NOUN

And in the evening, there are displays of _____ , such
                                              PLURAL NOUN

as Roman _____ , shooting _____ , and
             PLURAL NOUN   PLURAL NOUN

_____ rockets that _____ _____
  ADJECTIVE   ADVERB   VERB

the sky. A word of caution: Do not use _____ unless
                                            PLURAL NOUN

you are supervised by a knowledgeable _____ .
                                            NOUN

MAD LIBS® is fun to play with friends, but you can also play it by yourself! To begin with, DO NOT look at the story on the page below. Fill in the blanks on this page with the words called for. Then, using the words you have selected, fill in the blank spaces in the story.

Now you've created your own hilarious MAD LIBS® game!

FAMOUS QUOTES FROM THE AMERICAN REVOLUTION

NOUN _____

NOUN _____

COLOR _____

PART OF THE BODY (PLURAL) _____

NOUN _____

PLURAL NOUN _____

VERB ENDING IN "ING" _____

NOUN _____

PLURAL NOUN _____

PLURAL NOUN _____

ADJECTIVE _____

NOUN _____

MAD LIBS®
FAMOUS QUOTES FROM THE AMERICAN REVOLUTION

Nathan Hale said: "I regret that I have but one _____

NOUN

to give to my _____."

NOUN

William Prescott said: "Don't fire until you see the _____

COLOR

of their _____."

PART OF THE BODY (PLURAL)

Patrick Henry said: "Give me liberty or give me _____."

NOUN

Paul Revere said: "The _____ are _____."

PLURAL NOUN   VERB ENDING IN "ING"

John Hancock said: "I wrote my _____ large so the king

NOUN

could read it without his _____."

PLURAL NOUN

Thomas Jefferson said: "All _____ are created equal. They

PLURAL NOUN

are endowed by their creator with certain _____ rights

ADJECTIVE

and among these are life, liberty, and the pursuit of _____."

NOUN

MAD LIBS® is fun to play with friends, but you can also play it by yourself! To begin with, DO NOT look at the story on the page below. Fill in the blanks on this page with the words called for. Then, using the words you have selected, fill in the blank spaces in the story.

Now you've created your own hilarious MAD LIBS® game!

VOTING MADE EASY AS ONE, TWO, THREE

ADJECTIVE _____

VERB ENDING IN "ING" _____

PLURAL NOUN _____

NOUN _____

ADVERB _____

VERB ENDING IN "ING" _____

NOUN _____

VERB _____

NOUN _____

NOUN _____

VERB _____

NOUN _____

PART OF THE BODY _____

LETTER OF THE ALPHABET _____

NOUN _____

NOUN _____

EXCLAMATION _____

TYPE OF FOOD _____

VERB _____

NOUN _____

MAD LIBS
VOTING MADE EASY
AS ONE, TWO, THREE

Here are some very _____ instructions on how to vote,
ADJECTIVE

brought to you by the Citizens for _____ Awareness:
VERB ENDING IN "ING"

STEP 1: Sign in with one of the _____ at the registration
PLURAL NOUN

table. You may have to show them your _____ to
NOUN

prove your identity.

STEP 2: Proceed _____ to an available _____
ADVERB   VERB ENDING IN "ING"

booth. (Be sure to close the _____ behind you so that
NOUN

no one can watch you _____.)
VERB

STEP 3: How you vote varies from _____ to _____. In
NOUN   NOUN

some states, you _____ by pulling a/an _____
VERB   NOUN

with your _____. In others, you must mark a
PART OF THE BODY

ballot by placing a/an _____ in a small
LETTER OF THE ALPHABET

_____ opposite your candidate's _____.
NOUN   NOUN

"_____!" you will cry. "Voting's as easy as _____!"
EXCLAMATION   TYPE OF FOOD

So be sure to _____ on Election Day, because every _____
VERB   NOUN

counts!

MAD LIBS® is fun to play with friends, but you can also play it by yourself! To begin with, DO NOT look at the story on the page below. Fill in the blanks on this page with the words called for. Then, using the words you have selected, fill in the blank spaces in the story.

Now you've created your own hilarious MAD LIBS® game!

NUCLEAR TEST BAN TREATY AND A NEW LAW

A PLACE _____

PLURAL NOUN _____

PLURAL NOUN _____

PLURAL NOUN _____

ADJECTIVE_____

NOUN _____

NOUN _____

SAME NOUN_____

SAME NOUN_____

SAME NOUN_____

A PLACE _____

NUMBER _____

TYPE OF LIQUID _____

MAD LIBS®
NUCLEAR TEST BAN TREATY AND A NEW LAW

YOU HAVE WRITTEN A NUCLEAR TEST BAN TREATY

It is hereby agreed by the Big Three, the United States, Russia, and

_____, that there will be no further testing of nuclear
<u>A PLACE</u>

_____. However, tests may be made under _____.
<u>PLURAL NOUN</u>   <u>PLURAL NOUN</u>

Explosions must be limited to one-half megaton, which is equal to

500,000 tons of _____. We all agree that this sounds
<u>PLURAL NOUN</u>

_____ and is the only way to keep someone from blowing
<u>ADJECTIVE</u>

up the _____.
<u>NOUN</u>

YOU HAVE WRITTEN A NEW LAW

It will be unlawful to own a/an _____ or carry a concealed
<u>NOUN</u>

_____ without a/an _____ license. The penalty
<u>SAME NOUN</u>   <u>SAME NOUN</u>

for _____-carrying will be thirty days in the _____
<u>SAME NOUN</u>   <u>A PLACE</u>

or a fine of _____ dollars. The penalty is double if the person
<u>NUMBER</u>

is arrested while under the influence of _____.
<u>TYPE OF LIQUID</u>

MAD LIBS® is fun to play with friends, but you can also play it by yourself! To begin with, DO NOT look at the story on the page below. Fill in the blanks on this page with the words called for. Then, using the words you have selected, fill in the blank spaces in the story.

Now you've created your own hilarious MAD LIBS® game!

WHITE HOUSE TOUR

PLURAL NOUN _____

VERB _____

COLOR_____

ADJECTIVE_____

NOUN _____

NUMBER _____

NOUN _____

ADJECTIVE_____

PLURAL NOUN _____

PLURAL NOUN _____

VERB (PAST TENSE)_____

ROOM _____

FAMOUS PERSON_____

VERB ENDING IN "ING" _____

NOUN _____

NOUN _____

MAD LIBS
WHITE HOUSE TOUR

Ladies and _____ , please _____ this way as we begin
          PLURAL NOUN   VERB

our tour of the _____ House, _____ home of our nation's
              COLOR   ADJECTIVE

_____ . It has more than _____ rooms! The _____
  NOUN   NUMBER   NOUN

Room, where huge _____ _____ are held, is the
                 ADJECTIVE   PLURAL NOUN

largest. Throughout the mansion, you will find portraits of previous

_____ , who also _____ here. Upstairs, you can see
PLURAL NOUN   VERB (PAST TENSE)

the famous Lincoln _____ , where the ghost of _____
              ROOM   FAMOUS PERSON

has often been seen _____ . The president's
                  VERB ENDING IN "ING"

_____ is in the West Wing and is shaped like a/an _____ .
  NOUN   NOUN

MAD LIBS® is fun to play with friends, but you can also play it by yourself! To begin with, DO NOT look at the story on the page below. Fill in the blanks on this page with the words called for. Then, using the words you have selected, fill in the blank spaces in the story.

Now you've created your own hilarious MAD LIBS® game!

STATE OF THE UNION

ADJECTIVE_____

PLURAL NOUN _____

ADJECTIVE_____

NOUN _____

PLURAL NOUN _____

ADJECTIVE_____

ADJECTIVE_____

VERB ENDING IN "ING" _____

PLURAL NOUN _____

PLURAL NOUN _____

ADVERB_____

NOUN _____

NOUN _____

VERB _____

ADJECTIVE_____

PLURAL NOUN _____

ADVERB_____

VERB _____

ADJECTIVE_____

MAD LIBS®
STATE OF THE UNION

_____ evening, distinguished _____ , _____
ADJECTIVE   PLURAL NOUN   ADJECTIVE

senators, members of the Supreme _____ , my fellow
NOUN

_____ . I am _____ to announce that the state of our
PLURAL NOUN   ADJECTIVE

union is _____ ! Inflation is _____ to an all-
ADJECTIVE   VERB ENDING IN "ING"

time low. The test scores of our _____ are at an all-time high.
PLURAL NOUN

And, _____ are expanding _____ . However, the
PLURAL NOUN   ADVERB

Congress still refuses to pass _____ reform, or to increase the
NOUN

size of the _____ budget, or to _____ the bill governing
NOUN   VERB

our _____ national _____ . Tonight, I _____
ADJECTIVE   PLURAL NOUN   ADVERB

suggest that you _____ them a/an _____ letter or fax.
VERB   ADJECTIVE

MAD LIBS® is fun to play with friends, but you can also play it by yourself! To begin with, DO NOT look at the story on the page below. Fill in the blanks on this page with the words called for. Then, using the words you have selected, fill in the blank spaces in the story.

Now you've created your own hilarious MAD LIBS® game!

THE THREE BRANCHES OF GOVERNMENT

PLURAL NOUN _____

NOUN _____

PLURAL NOUN _____

ADJECTIVE_____

PLURAL NOUN _____

OCCUPATION _____

VERB ENDING IN "S"_____

VERB ENDING IN "ING" _____

NOUN _____

VERB (PAST TENSE)_____

NOUN _____

ADJECTIVE_____

PLURAL NOUN _____

PLURAL NOUN _____

PLURAL NOUN _____

OCCUPATION _____

MAD LIBS
THE THREE BRANCHES OF GOVERNMENT

Our founding _____ designed our _____ with three
         PLURAL NOUN   NOUN

main branches. This was to protect the _____ from a/an
                                              PLURAL NOUN

_____ leader. The three branches form a system of checks
   ADJECTIVE

and _____ .
        PLURAL NOUN

THE EXECUTIVE BRANCH includes the office of _____ .
                                                      OCCUPATION

This branch _____ the judicial and legislative branches
              VERB ENDING IN "S"

and has _____ power.
          VERB ENDING IN "ING"

THE JUDICIAL BRANCH is responsible for upholding the _____ ,
                                                          NOUN

which was _____ by our founding fathers. The Judicial
            VERB (PAST TENSE)

Branch includes a Supreme _____ , which rules on _____
                              NOUN   ADJECTIVE

issues.

THE LEGISLATIVE BRANCH is divided into two _____ — the
                                               PLURAL NOUN

Congress and the Senate. Together they regulate which _____
                                                          PLURAL NOUN

are passed into _____ . This branch, however, can be vetoed
                  PLURAL NOUN

by the _____ .
          OCCUPATION

MAD LIBS® is fun to play with friends, but you can also play it by yourself! To begin with, DO NOT look at the story on the page below. Fill in the blanks on this page with the words called for. Then, using the words you have selected, fill in the blank spaces in the story.

Now you've created your own hilarious MAD LIBS® game!

IMPEACHMENT

NOUN _____

NOUN _____

ADVERB _____

VERB _____

PLURAL NOUN _____

ADJECTIVE _____

PLURAL NOUN _____

ADJECTIVE _____

SAME AS FIRST NOUN _____

PLURAL NOUN _____

NOUN _____

ADJECTIVE _____

ADVERB _____

PLURAL NOUN _____

PART OF THE BODY (PLURAL) _____

ADJECTIVE _____

SAME ADJECTIVE _____

MAD LIBS
IMPEACHMENT

A/An _____ can be impeached for any number of reasons,
     NOUN

including lying to the United States _____ , _____
                   NOUN   ADVERB

abusing his powers to _____ _____ , making
               VERB   PLURAL NOUN

_____ remarks regarding _____ , or otherwise
   ADJECTIVE   PLURAL NOUN

behaving in a/an _____ manner. If the _____ is
       ADJECTIVE   SAME AS FIRST NOUN

impeached by the House of _____ , a trial in the Senate could
               PLURAL NOUN

follow, presided over by the Chief _____ of the _____
               NOUN   ADJECTIVE

Court. After _____ weighing the _____ , senators
       ADVERB   PLURAL NOUN

will raise their _____ and cast a vote of either
      PART OF THE BODY (PLURAL)

" _____ !" or "not _____ !"
  ADJECTIVE   SAME ADJECTIVE

MAD LIBS® is fun to play with friends, but you can also play it by yourself! To begin with, DO NOT look at the story on the page below. Fill in the blanks on this page with the words called for. Then, using the words you have selected, fill in the blank spaces in the story.

Now you've created your own hilarious MAD LIBS® game!

THE "CHECKERS" SPEECH

PLURAL NOUN _____

VERB _____

OCCUPATION _____

NOUN _____

NOUN _____

NOUN _____

VERB (PAST TENSE) _____

ADVERB _____

NOUN _____

ADJECTIVE _____

SAME NOUN _____

ADJECTIVE _____

ADJECTIVE _____

ANIMAL _____

NOUN _____

VERB _____

MAD LIBS®
THE "CHECKERS" SPEECH

My fellow _____ , I _____ before you tonight as a
          PLURAL NOUN   VERB

candidate for _____ , and as a man whose _____ and
             OCCUPATION   NOUN

_____ have been questioned. Every _____ that Pat and
  NOUN   NOUN

I have ever _____ is _____ ours. Pat doesn't have
        VERB (PAST TENSE)   ADVERB

a mink _____ , but she does have a/an _____ Republican
     NOUN   ADJECTIVE

cloth _____ . I always tell her she would look
          SAME NOUN

_____ in anything. We did get one gift, however. It was a/an
ADJECTIVE

_____ cocker spaniel _____ , and our little _____ ,
ADJECTIVE   ANIMAL   NOUN

Tricia, named it Checkers. And no matter what they say, we're going

to _____ it.
   VERB

MAD LIBS® is fun to play with friends, but you can also play it by yourself! To begin with, DO NOT look at the story on the page below. Fill in the blanks on this page with the words called for. Then, using the words you have selected, fill in the blank spaces in the story.

Now you've created your own hilarious MAD LIBS® game!

DEMOCRATS

ADJECTIVE _____

PLURAL NOUN _____

PLURAL NOUN _____

VERB ENDING IN "ING" _____

NOUN _____

VERB _____

SAME NOUN _____

NOUN BEGINNING WITH "H" _____

NOUN _____

NOUN _____

VERB _____

PLURAL NOUN _____

PART OF THE BODY (PLURAL) _____

ADJECTIVE _____

NOUN _____

MAD LIBS
DEMOCRATS

Democrats believe in _____ rights for _____, large
$\qquad$ ADJECTIVE $\qquad$ PLURAL NOUN

government _____, and _____ the environment.
$\qquad$ PLURAL NOUN $\qquad$ VERB ENDING IN "ING"

Famous Democrats include Franklin Roosevelt, who said, "The only

_____ we have to _____ is _____ itself," and
NOUN $\qquad$ VERB $\qquad$ SAME NOUN

Harry Truman, whose nickname was "Give 'em _____
$\qquad$ NOUN BEGINNING WITH "H"

Harry." Truman made famous the phrase: "The _____ stops here!"
$\qquad$ NOUN

Democrats often have the support of _____ unions, people
$\qquad$ NOUN

who _____ in big cities, and famous Hollywood _____.
VERB $\qquad$ PLURAL NOUN

The symbol for the Democrats is the donkey — an animal with long

_____, a/an _____ laugh, and a floppy _____.
PART OF THE BODY (PLURAL) $\qquad$ ADJECTIVE $\qquad$ NOUN

MAD LIBS® is fun to play with friends, but you can also play it by yourself! To begin with, DO NOT look at the story on the page below. Fill in the blanks on this page with the words called for. Then, using the words you have selected, fill in the blank spaces in the story.

Now you've created your own hilarious MAD LIBS® game!

REPUBLICANS

ADJECTIVE _____

PLURAL NOUN _____

VERB ENDING IN "ING" _____

ADJECTIVE _____

NOUN _____

CITY _____

ADJECTIVE _____

NOUN _____

ADJECTIVE STARTING WITH "G" _____

ADJECTIVE STARTING WITH "O" _____

NOUN STARTING WITH "P" _____

PLURAL NOUN _____

PLURAL NOUN _____

ANIMAL _____

MAD LIBS
REPUBLICANS

Republicans believe in a/an _____ military, lower
                                           ADJECTIVE

_____, and _____ in school. The first
        PLURAL NOUN   VERB ENDING IN "ING"

Republican president was " _____ "Abe Lincoln. He kept the
                                        ADJECTIVE

_____ together during the Civil War and delivered the
              NOUN

historical _____ Address. Another Republican president was
                  CITY

" _____ "Dick Nixon. He's famous for saying, "I am not a/an
       ADJECTIVE

_____." Another name for the Republican Party is the G.O.P.,
       NOUN

which stands for _____ _____
                     ADJECTIVE STARTING WITH "G"   ADJECTIVE STARTING WITH "O"

_____. They also believe that _____ have
    NOUN STARTING WITH "P"   PLURAL NOUN

the right to make their own _____. The symbol of the
                                      PLURAL NOUN

Republican Party is the _____.
                                 ANIMAL

From MAD LIBS® FOR PRESIDENT • Copyright © 2004, 2000 by Price Stern Sloan,
a division of Penguin Young Readers Group, 345 Hudson Street, New York, New York 10014.

MAD LIBS® is fun to play with friends, but you can also play it by yourself! To begin with, DO NOT look at the story on the page below. Fill in the blanks on this page with the words called for. Then, using the words you have selected, fill in the blank spaces in the story.

Now you've created your own hilarious MAD LIBS® game!

A TYPICAL HISTORY TEST

NOUN _____

PLURAL NOUN _____

CITY _____

NOUN _____

PLURAL NOUN _____

PLURAL NOUN _____

COUNTRY _____

NOUN _____

ADJECTIVE_____

PERSON IN ROOM (MALE)_____

CELEBRITY (MALE) _____

CELEBRITY (MALE) _____

VERB ENDING IN "ING" _____

CELEBRITY (MALE)_____

FAMOUS DISCOVERY_____

CELEBRITY (FEMALE) _____

MAD LIBS®

A TYPICAL HISTORY TEST

Instructions: When the _____ *rings, unfold your papers and*
$\qquad$ NOUN

answer the following _____ .
$\qquad$ PLURAL NOUN

1. What general won the Battle of _____?
   $\qquad$ CITY

2. Which American _____ said, "Give me liberty or give me
   $\qquad$ NOUN

   _____"?
   PLURAL NOUN

3. Who was the first president of the United _____ of _____?
   $\qquad$ PLURAL NOUN $\qquad$ COUNTRY

4. Why did Benjamin Franklin fly a/an _____ during a
   $\qquad$ NOUN

   thunderstorm?

5. Who made the first _____ flag?
   $\qquad$ ADJECTIVE

Answers to test:

1. _____ .
   PERSON IN ROOM (MALE)

2. _____ , when he was executed by _____
   CELEBRITY (MALE) $\qquad$ CELEBRITY (MALE)

   for _____ .
   VERB ENDING IN "ING"

3. _____
   CELEBRITY (MALE)

4. He was discovering _____ .
   FAMOUS DISCOVERY

5. _____
   CELEBRITY (FEMALE)

MAD LIBS® is fun to play with friends, but you can also play it by yourself! To begin with, DO NOT look at the story on the page below. Fill in the blanks on this page with the words called for. Then, using the words you have selected, fill in the blank spaces in the story.

Now you've created your own hilarious MAD LIBS® game!

YANKEE DOODLE _____
NOUN

ADJECTIVE_____

VERB _____

SAME NOUN_____

VERB _____

RELATIVE _____

PERSON IN ROOM (MALE)_____

HOLIDAY_____

NOUN _____

NOUN _____

A PLACE _____

ANIMAL _____

NOUN _____

MAD LIBS

YANKEE DOODLE _____
                        NOUN

(Here's a really _____ tune that everybody knows. You can
                     ADJECTIVE

_____ it on the Fourth of July or Presidents' Day!)
   VERB

I'm a Yankee Doodle _____.
                         SAME NOUN

Yankee Doodle do or _____.
                         VERB

A real live _____ of my Uncle _____.
              RELATIVE   PERSON IN ROOM (MALE)

Born on _____.
           HOLIDAY

I've got a Yankee Doodle _____.
                              NOUN

She's my Yankee Doodle _____.
                             NOUN

Yankee Doodle went to _____.
                          A PLACE

Just to ride a/an _____.
                      ANIMAL

I am that Yankee Doodle _____.
                             NOUN